Say it in Scots

SCOTTISH WEATHER

Say it in Scots

SCOTTISH WEATHER

Chris Robinson &
Eileen Finlayson

BLACK & WHITE PUBLISHING

First published 2008
by Black & White Publishing Ltd
99 Giles Street, Edinburgh EH6 6BZ

ISBN: 978 1 84502 194 8

1 3 5 7 9 10 8 6 4 2   08 09 10 11 12

Copyright © Chris Robinson and Eileen Finlayson, 2008
Illustrations by Garry Thorburn
www.caricaturecards.co.uk

A CIP catalogue record for this book is available from the British Library.

Typeset by Ellipsis Books Ltd
Printed and bound by Nørhaven Paperback A/S

Contents

Say it in Scots

~~~~~~~~~~~~~~~~~~~~~~~~

Whether you are a Scots speaker already, or whether you are a visitor to Scotland, this series of books is guaranteed to awaken your enthusiasm for the Scots language. There is bound to be something in these books to interest you. They are based on the *Scottish National Dictionary* and *A Dictionary of the Older Scottish Tongue*, which are now available online as the *Dictionary of the Scots Language* at **www.dsl.ac.uk.** Additional material comes from the ongoing research of Scottish Language Dictionaries, who are responsible for the stewardship of these great reference works and for keeping the record of Scots words up to date.

Scots is the language of Lowland Scotland and the Northern Isles. It is also used in parts of Ulster. Along with English and Gaelic, it is one of Scotland's three indigenous languages. Scots is descended from

Northern Old English, itself greatly influenced by Old Scandinavian. From the twelfth century onwards, it became increasingly established in Lowland Scotland and was then enriched by words borrowed from French, Latin, Gaelic and Dutch. It was the language of government, spoken by kings, courtiers, poets and the people. It has a literary heritage the equal of any in Europe.

Like any other language, it has its own dialects such as Glaswegian, Ayrshire, Shetland, Doric, Border Scots, etc. These have a rich diversity and share a central core uniting them as varieties of the Scots language. We have tried to reflect the history and variety of Scots in these books and hope you will find some words that you can savour on your tongue and slip into everyday conversation.

Some of the spelling, especially in the older quotations, may be unfamiliar, but if you try reading the quotations out loud, you will find they are not difficult to understand.

Chris Robinson

Director

Scottish Language Dictionaries

www.scotsdictionaries.org.uk

Introduction

Scotland's climate is remarkable for its infinite variety
throughout the year. In spite of Robert Wanlock's
assertion in his *Moorland Rhymes* that *There's three
months o' bluister tae ilk' ane o' sun*, there are sunny
days in Scotland at every season. In summer there are
days when a haze ripples above the grass and the sound
of droning insects is punctuated by the cracking of broom
seedpods in the heat. But at high latitudes the sun is not
always particularly warm and the weather can change in
moments. In winter, sunny days and clear, starry skies at
night bring frosty weather and, sometimes, a clear view
of the *aurora borealis*. Even hard frosts do not usually
persist for long periods in Lowland Scotland. Surrounded
by sea except on the English border, Scotland's climate
is generally temperate, a fact noticed by Julius Caesar,

if J. Leslie's *The Historie of Scotland* translated by
J. Dalrymple (1596) is to be believed:

> *Caesar said, he fand heit and calde less vehement*
> *in Scotlande than in France.*

So be prepared with your sunscreen, a thick sweater and
your wellington boots for four seasons in one Scottish
day.

1 Rain and Hail

Scotland and Ireland are the first dropping-off places for moisture swept in by winds from the Atlantic Ocean. No wonder then that they are both richly green countries, even at the height of summer. Nor is it surprising that the Scots language has a huge vocabulary of words for all the different kinds of precipitation that make our weather so varied and interesting.

Rain can *smirr, teem, stot, come doon in stair rods, no tak time tae come doon* or *come doon hale* [whole] *watter*. It can *rain auld wives and pipe staples* as well as *cats and dogs*.

There can be an *onding*, a *plump*, a *plype*, a *scudder* or a *blatter*. Less dramatically, sometimes the weather is just *plowtery*, with a *spitter* or a *dreep* or a *dribble*.

Here is a selection of words to describe most degrees of humidity you are likely to experience.

Black weet – a deluge of rain.

Blatter – to rattle, beat violently (often used of rain or hail); a violent rain or hailstorm. A period of sunshine during unsettled weather, or a moment of joy in troubled times may pessimistically be called
   the blink afore the blatter.

So, if you feel moved to put a dampener on other people's happiness, shake your head sagely and say
   Ay, ay, it winnae last – it's jist the blink afore the blatter.

Blashy – rainy, wet, gusty. Blashy weather is not just unpleasant, it can have gruesome consequences for shepherds:

> *The thick blawn Wreaths* [drifts] *of Snaw, or blashy Thows* [thaws], *May smoor* [smother] *your Wathers* [castrated male sheep], *and may rot your Ews.*

> (ALLAN RAMSAY *The Gentle Shepherd* 1725)

Blaw bye – a passing shower. Literally, this is rain that is just blowing by in the wind. It can also be used figuratively of a quick outburst of anger. At least there is room for optimism here. You know it won't last.

Deval – stop; halt. Although this is a general word that can be applied to the cessation of any activity, it is most usually applied to rain or snow and can be used as a verb or a noun.

Dreep – a light steady fall of rain.

Dreich – Scotland's favourite weather word! The *ch* is pronounced as the throaty sound in *loch*. If you do not have this sound in your language, you may hear it as *k*, and *loch* and *lock* will sound identical to you. If you have this problem, try pronouncing *dreich* and *loch* as though they ended with a strong *h* sound and you will get quite close to the correct pronunciation. Once you can do that, you will be able to train your ears to hear the sound. You will also improve your Dutch and German accent for names such as van Gogh, Bach and Munich.

Sheena Blackhall in *Wittgenstein's Web* (1996) enthuses:

> *Nae Inglis wird alane can convoy the multiplicity o thocht ahin thon ae wird dreich. Dreich is a cauld, mochy, jeelin, dowie wird — a wird fur weather, character, emotion: an yon's bit scartit the tap o't, fur there's a guid gowpenfu o the eldritch steered inno't anna.*

[No English word alone can convey the multiplicity of thought behind that one word dreich. Dreich is a cold, clammy, chilling, depressing word – a word for weather, character, emotion: and that's but scratched the surface of it, for there's a good double handful of the supernatural stirred into it as well].

Dreich can be all of these things. It can also mean dry as dust (as in a dreich sermon) and with reference to weather may suggest anything and everything from merely overcast to distinctly damp, but it always carries a burden of utter joylessness.

Dribble – drizzle.

Drouk – to soak.

Most often appearing as *droukit,* the word *drouk* is not easily translatable. It does not simply mean to soak through. It also contains the inner misery and the outer bedraggled appearance. The simile *as weet as a droukit rat* conveys some of the pathos that attaches to a good droukin. As this chapter implies, if you stand outside long enough you are guaranteed to find out the meaning of droukit for yourself.

Drouth – prolonged or extreme dry weather; drought. In contrast to the plethora of words for rain, this is one of the very few Scots words for lack of rain.

However, even in Scotland, water shortages are nothing new. In 1580, the Edinburgh Records note

The scarcenes of watter . . . in the drowth and somer seasoun;

and in 1613 we read in the Aberdeen Ecclesiastical Records of

The extraordinarie drouth quhilk [which] *is liklie to burne wp* [up] *and destroy the cornis.*

It was believed that a period of drought could encourage the spread of plague:

The said pest . . . rais be excessive hetis [heatwaves] *and drouth*

(JOHN BELLENDEN *Livy's History of Rome* 1533)

This is not an unreasonable belief as such hot, dry

conditions are ideal for breeding the fleas which carry the pest [plague].

Drouth can also mean thirst. In Robert Burns' poem, *Tam o' Shanter*, Tam drinks with Souter Johnny, *His ancient, trusted, drouthy crony*, and a drinker's drouth is one of the effects of over-indulgence that they probably both suffered from the following morning.

Housewives welcome a good drouth on wash-day, as the clothes on the line will dry quickly. Here it does not necessarily mean prolonged dryness but may refer more to a good drying wind combined with a temporary lack of actual rain.

Drowie – misty, drizzling, damp. These two quotations show how large a part attitude plays in appreciation of the weather. Who would wish to venture *On yon grey drowy muir Whaur snell* [biting] *blasts scour ye ti the bane?* (*Scots Magazine* August 1929). On the other hand, the next quotation conveys a feeling of relief that the rain is not excessive:

It was a dull, drowy (showery) sort of day, not a

*rain, but a Scotch mist, a wee damp as they express
it in those parts*

(Kelso Chronicle 1 January 1915)

Fair – fair; to become fair after rain, sleet or snow.
In Scots, fair can be used as a verb and so you might
venture out if it fairs.

Feechie – foul, dirty, rainy and puddly. Feechie can
be used for anything messy and unpleasant. Feech! is an
exclamation of disgust.

Growin shoorie – a welcome shower to help the
young crops grow. We find this in Mary Johnston's *Ryen*
[rain] (2007), which she prefaces with a North-East
saying:

Dinna fash, ryen winna ging faarer than yer skin.
[Don't worry, rain won't go further than your skin.]

*Spirken, spitten, drappie weet,
growin shoories, poor doons.*

hale waater, teemin ryen,
thunder plumps, ondyngs.

Bit, smoocherin, smirr, smaa weet
daats [caresses] *yer face wi smeerichs,* [kisses]
hings diamonds on yer winkers, [eyelashes]
spairges [scatters] *opals in yer hair.*

Haar – see under **Wind and Storm.**

Hail – like many Scots words, this one is shared with English with no difference in the pronunciation, although there may be some variation in the spelling in older texts:

Schouris of haill can fra the North discend.

(ROBERT HENRYSON *The Testament of Cresseid* c.1500)

Liddesdale drow – a thick, wetting drizzle such as might be experienced in the Borders valley of Liddesdale.

I have heard an old lady remark, quoting a

local saw: "A Liddesdul drow Weets a Tibidull
[Teviotdale] *man Throw and throw"*

(*Border Magazine* August 1933)

Mochy – close, humid. Mochy is pronounced with the *ch* representing the throaty Scots sound as described for **dreich.** Like dreich, this word can have a range of meanings, but mochy invariably implies a high level of humidity. It is perhaps most often used to capture in a single word the feeling of damp, close, muggy, misty and oppressive weather. An Argyllshire quotation from the *English Dialect Dictionary* seems to suggest an early date for the word:

I' the time o' the Flood the deil gaed sailin' by the
Ark on a barn-door, an' said, "It's a mochy mornin,
mester Noah".

However, the earliest recorded use actually comes from Gavin Douglas in his *Aeneid* of 1513, where he refers to

moich hailsum stovys
[damp health-giving vapours].

The early Scottish lexicographer, John Jamieson (1825) observes

> *that mochy is not applied to mist indiscriminately;*
> *but to that only which is produced by great heat, or*
> *an accompaniment of it, when the air is so close as*
> *to affect the organs of respiration.*

However, 'great heat' is relative and can refer both to the thundery heat of summer or to unseasonable warmth in winter, accompanied by high humidity.

Mochy can also be used to describe the condition of corn or other foodstuffs which have been spoilt by damp and heat and, as this quotation from the *Aberdeen Evening Express* (8 October 1998) about a stench in a block of flats shows, it can even refer to smell:

> *It's a vile, mochy smell like something is rotting.*

So, the next clammy, dreepin day that comes along, when your oxters [armpits] feel or smell a bit mochy, you have just the word you need.

Onding – a heavy, fall of rain or snow, a downpour. Ding is a verb meaning to beat or strike with heavy blows. So a real onding of rain has some force behind it. Onding can be used figuratively to mean an assault, attack, onset, outburst of noise, talk, etc. as in

The on-ding of their ill tongues

(SAMUEL CROCKETT *The Raiders* 1893)

and

The anger o' a king is like the on-ding o' daith itsel.

(T. W. PATERSON *The Wyse-Sayin's o' Solomon* 1916)

More cheerily:

At streek o' day [daybreak], *ae canty* [pleasant]
Spring, Tam wauken'd [wakened] *to the birds'
onding.*

(JOHN HORNE *A Lan'wart Loon* 1928)

Oorlich – damp, chilly and unpleasant, raw, bleak, depressing.

[16]

Oorlich shoo'ers o' drift an' hail

(WILLIAM ALEXANDER *Johnny Gibb* 1871)

If you are caught in oorlich weather, you might be a bit oorlich yourself, damp and miserable. There might even be just a hint of the supernatural in the word. So if you are hurrying home in an oorlich night – don't look behind you!

Peuch, peuchle – to rain or snow lightly in fits and starts. Another word with *ch* as in **dreich**. It can be used of people in the sense of puffing and peuchin or peuchlin for want of breath.

Plover, pluvar – plover. This word derives from Old French *plovier* and Latin *pluvius,* which mean
to do with rain.

The plover is the rain bird because the arrival of migratory flocks often coincides with the autumn rains. Once a delicacy, plovers appear in the *Stirling Palace Larder*

Book of 1597 and an Act of 1555 provides
> *That na poutis* [poults, young game birds] *pertrik*
> [partridge] *pluwer . . . be slane vnto the feist of*
> *Michaelmes.*

Plowtery – messy, dirty wet, showery.

Plump – a sudden heavy fall of rain. See
Thunderplump.

Plype – a sudden downpour or, more generally, any
sudden soaking. This onomatopoeic word could be
applied a to solid sheet of rain that *disnae tak time tae
come doon*:
> *There was a plype o' rain falling at the time*
> (LORD ERNEST HAMILTON *The Outlaws of the Marches* 1897).

However, a plype can on occasion be welcome:
> *Cheese an' breed washen doon wi plipes o' caal*
> *watter.*

> (WILLIAM MILNE *Eppie Elrick* 1955)

Rouk – mist or sea-fog, drizzle. There is something very bleak, if poetic, about this word, brought to us through the rouks of time by the Vikings.

Mair scouthry like it still does look,
At length comes on in mochy rook.

(GEORGE ROBERTSON Har'st Rig 1786)

The peculiar fog . . . is called in some parts of
Scotland the ground rook, and strongly resembles a
thick smoke arising from the surface of the earth.

(R. KERR General View of the Agriculture of the County of
Berwick 1809)

Saft – soft, gentle (of rain). On a saft day, on a Scottish mountain, turn your face up to the saft rain and feel it doing your complexion a world of good. *Tait's Edinburgh Magazine* (1842) captures the tone:

A close drizzling rain . . . which the waiter assured
me was "a fine saft drappin' wather."

Scudder – a driving shower of rain or snow, to rain in

a windy blast. To scud means both to travel rapidly and to administer a thrashing. Both of these meanings are carried into scudder.

During the past week we have experienced some gey caul' scudders.

(Huntly Express 22 July 1949)

Anyone who has ever waited at an Edinburgh bus-stop on a rainy day, with an outside-in umbrella, will recognise

A scudderin'-dudderin' wund blawin' doon the street.

(Scots Magazine July 1897)

Scuddrie, scouthry – marked by cold, driving showers of rain or snow:

Sae, as auld Boreas 'gan to blow, Spitting out scuddrie sleet an' snow.

(ALEXANDER HARPER Fruits of Solitary Hours 1852)

Shoor, shour – shower.

Shore – to threaten. If it isn't shorin rain, it's probably raining already.

Simmer-lunts – moisture at sunrise. These are the pretty wisps of mist that rise from lochs, rivers and trees with the first warmth of the morning.

Simmer-sob – a period of frequent slight rain-showers in early summer, especially in May.

> *Yon summer sob is out. This night looks well ...*
>
> (ALEXANDER ROSS *Helenore; or The Fortunate Shepherdess* 1768)

Smirr – a fine rain, drizzle, smoke, haze. Some kinds of rain seem wetter than others and a smirr creeps damply and deviously in below umbrellas. The pervasiveness of smirring rain is captured by Alan Sharp:

> *When she got out it was starting to rain a soft smirr.*
> *... The rain spun down all around her, soundless,*
> *small as small, a mood of rain falling gently yet*
> *relentlessly, wetting everywhere.*
>
> (ALAN SHARP *A Green Tree in Gedde* 1965)

Sharp's phrase 'a mood of rain' will resonate with anyone who has sat in a smirr gazing at a romantic ruin or a mountain landscape. Ian Rankin is another fan of this word:

> The Scots language is especially rich in words to do with the weather: 'dreich' and 'smirr' are only two of them . . . Only it wasn't real rain, it was smirr, a fine spray-mist which drenched you before you knew it. It was blowing in from the west, moisture straight from the Atlantic Ocean. It was all Rebus needed first thing on a dreich Monday morning.
>
> (IAN RANKIN *Black and Blue* 1997)

Rebus might not appreciate a smirr, but if we must have rain this is a pleasantly gentle kind to have.

Spitter – a slight shower of rain or snow.

Stot – to bounce. Hailstones stot. The phrase 'stottin rain' conjures up a vivid picture of rain hitting the ground with considerable force.

Teem – to pour, to empty. Although this word has become obsolete in Standard English south of the border, it is still often used in Scots and some dialects of English. You can teem the tatties [potatoes], or, with a warning cry of *gardyloo!*, you can teem your chamberpot into the street as the citizens of Edinburgh used to do. Most commonly, though, it is used of that kind of downpour when the heavens seem to open and rain teems down.

Thunderplump, thunnerplump – cloudburst:
> *Another thunderplump cascaded down on*
> *Gribben just as he was about to hit his tee shot at*
> *the tenth*

> (*Belfast News Letter* 5 June 1999)

so do not let any overkeen golfer tell you that
> *it never rains on the golf course!*

The *Sunday Mail* (11 August 2002) reads:
> *Drive into town with Mum who looks at the*
> *rivers of water running down the pavement and*

[23]

announces "Och, there's been a thunder plump".
A what? A thunderplump, she says, is what people
from the north-east call a sudden downpour . . .
great expression.

In spite of what 'Mum' in this quotation says, the expression is used widely throughout Scotland.

Weet – wet. This can be used as a verb (with the past tense *wat*), as a noun, or as an adjective.

According to Gabriel Setoun in *The Skipper of Barncraig* (1901):

People who live by the seaside distinguish between
a 'saut weet' and a 'fresh weet'. To be soaked with
rain might bring on an attack of rheumatism, but
after falling into the harbour, one might let his
clothes dry on him without the risk of a chill.

The Scots are a nation not given to exaggeration. Accustomed to occasional extremes of weather, they manage *to keep a calm souch* as this anecdote from the

Aberdeen Evening Express (2 August 1958) convincingly demonstrates:

> There is the classic story, too, of the man clinging to the wreckage of a shed being swept down the Dee who called out to a farmer as he whirled past, "Aye, min [man], it's a gey [rather] weetie day!"

With global warming, there is a strong possibility that the weather in Scotland will get milder and even wetter. Altogether more mochy. The words in this chapter are therefore likely to become increasingly useful. On the other hand, the words in the next chapter may be consigned to history.

2 Snow and Frost

You've been very preceese wi your wark, John Frost,
Altho ye hae wrocht [laboured] *in the dark, John*
Frost;
For ilka fit-stap frae the door to the slap [gap in the
fence]
Is braw as a new linen sark [shirt], *John Frost.*

(WILLIAM MILLER)

Snow and frost may look very beautiful and a cold, crisp winter may be healthier than a mild, mochy one but, as many of the quotations in this chapter remind us, for shepherds and others who work outside, winter is a hard and dangerous time.

Snow

Blin(d) drift – a white-out, a blinding snowstorm. Being out in a real blin drift is a frightening and dangerous experience. It is easy to lose all sense of direction, as any light there is seems to come from everywhere and visibility is reduced to a few feet. The second-best thing to do is to dig a snow hole and sit it out until the weather clears. The best thing to do is to stay at home.

Fann – a snow drift.

Feeding storm – bad weather that grows in intensity to add to what has gone before (especially of snow storms).

> *The weather here seems setting in for a feeding*
> *storm as we call it when the snow lies so long*
> (*The Letters of Sir Walter Scott* 1815)

A **stock storm** is another name for the same set of circumstances.

Flaggie – in large flakes (of snow). So, we might alliteratively improve on Robert Bridges' famous poem. *When men were all asleep the snow came flying, In flaggie flakes falling on the city brown . . .*

Flaucht, flauchin, flicht – a snowflake. Poor wee sheep!

> *Sair pinch'd for food, they lick the flaughts o' snaw,*
> *An' loudly bleat till a' the storm's awa'.*
> (*Weekly Magazine Or Edinburgh Amusement* 1 January 1778).

It is not only Robert Bridges who observed the onset of snow in the city:

> *Some fell* [very] *big flauchins o' snaw began to*

gently settle doon on the dry pavement.

(ALICK BLAIR *Rantin Robin and Marget* 1896)

Glaister – a thin covering of snow or ice. On a glaisterie day, the snow doesn't lie. It just falls and melts.

Grime – to sprinkle. You can tell winter is on the way when there is a grimin o snaw on the hills.

Mogs – to trudge laboriously through snow. Somehow, to mogs carries both the silence of snow and the effort of plodding through it:

. . . *mogsan heem* [home] *At'rou'* [through] *the snaw wi' hungry weem* [belly]

(WALTER DENNISON *The Orcadian Sketch-Book* 1880)

She spun me lies, did the tinkler wife,
But the roads slept under the snaw
An' misery mogsed knee-deep in her een [eyes],
So I couldna drive her awa'

(*Weekly Scotsman* 6 April 1929)

Moor – a dense fall of fine powdery snow liable to pile up into drifts. This is a word from Orkney and Shetland.

> *A moor had fa'n a' the heel* [whole] *day.*
>
> <div align="right">(WALTER DENNISON <i>The Orcadian Sketch-Book</i> 1880)</div>

The choking sense associated with powdery snow can also be used to describe nasal tubes choked with phlegm, so *mooran wi the cauld* in Orkney means that your nose is all blocked up with a cold.

Moorkavie – a blinding snowstorm, to snow heavily. This is another Shetland word.

> *Wi da snaa moorie-kaavie'n it ye widna a seen a skorie* [a young black-backed gull] *apo' da stemheid* [prow of the boat]
>
> <div align="right">(<i>Shetland Times</i> 14 March 1931)</div>

Again we are reminded of the dangers of weather:

> *Nae waanderin da hills wi' a moorcavie proogin*

[poking] *inta every fan* [snowdrift] *fur karcages*
[carcases].

(JOSEPH GRAY *Lowrie* 1949)

Saint Causlan's Flaw – a snowstorm in March.
Notes and Queries of 1850 records that this expression
was used in Angus where the parish church of Dunnichen
is situated. This church is dedicated to St Causlan
(Constantine), whose festival was held in March.

Skalva – soft flaky snow. This is a Shetland word. The
New Shetlander paints a vivid picture:

> *Kittiwakes began flying by in groups and presently
> they filled the air thick as a shower of skalva.*

(*New Shetlander* 1953)

Skift, skiff – to move lightly; a light shower of rain
or snow.

Skirr – to scurry; to whizz about. This word appears

in a novel but practical way of measuring snowfall in this conversation:

> "Have you had any snow yet?" "Only some skirrin sleets – no aneuch [enough] to track a hare"
>
> (JOHN WILSON *Noctes Ambrosianae* 1827)

Sleit, slete – sleet:

> The Vatter of Tay be veittis and sleit vaxit so great . . .
>
> (*The Chronicle of Perth* 1615 ed. James Maidment 1831)

This Older Scots example shows one of the eccentricities of Scots scribes. There was a lot of interchange in the use of *w*, *v* and *u*. In seventeenth-century England, *u* was regularly kept for the middle of words like moue [move] and house, *v* was used at the start of words like *vp* (up) and *vine* and *w* was used pretty much wherever you might expect it to be. Such spelling conventions did not catch on to the same extent with Scots scribes and they made liberal and erratic use of *w* into the bargain, causing in Scots manuscripts much greater variation than in English manuscripts of the same period. So from this quotation we deduce that the Water of Tay waxed by wet weather and sleet.

The next quotation manages to encapsulate the cutting pain sleet can inflict on bare skin when driven by the wind:

Scharpe soppys [densely packed masses] of sleit

(GAVIN DOUGLAS Aeneid (Prologue) 1513)

Smuir – to be choked, stifled, suffocated, to suffer or die from want of air (especially to perish by being buried in a snowdrift).

James Hogg, the writer known as the Ettrick Shepherd, in The Shepherd's Guide (1807) had little sympathy for shepherds who allowed their sheep to die in the snow. He says that smooring is occasioned solely by the shepherd's not having his flocks gathered to proper shelter. Nevertheless, it seems to have happened often enough and according to John Hunter's The Retrospect of an Artist's Life (1868), the year of the Big Snaw (1795) had its histories of smoorings of sheep.

Sometimes the shepherds themselves were the

victims; Robert Wilson (1822) tells of

How shepherds smoor'd amang the snaw.

Snaw – snow. Sir David Lindsay gives us an apt definition in *The Complaynte of Scotland* (1549):

The snau is ane congelit rane.

Something extremely unlikely is said to be as common as blue snaw – a bit like flying pigs that are spotted once in a blue moon. If someone does something exceptional you might say

There will be blue snaw the day [today].

Snaw-bree – melted snow in rivers; slush. Bree is liquid. It is often used of the liquid in which something has been steeped or cooked, containing the essence of that substance. If snaw-bree can be said to contain the essence of snow, it is in the temperature; nothing is colder on the feet than standing in snaw-bree.

Spindrift – sea spray whipped up by gusts of wind

and driven across the tops of the waves or snow blown up from the ground in swirls by gusts of wind, driving snow. The force of wind and sea is vividly described by John Galt in *The Entail* (1823):

> *The ocean boiling with tremendous violence, and the 'spindrift' rising like steam.*

The usage of spindrift from snow is attested by William Knight in *Auld Yule* (1869):

> *Now the snaw in spune-drift flew.*

Stock storm – bad weather that grows in intensity to add to what has gone before (especially of snow storms) This is another name for a **feeding storm**.

Swither – rush, swirl, flurry (of rain or snow):

> *Dan* [then] *a flann* [gust] *cam howlin doon an a swidder o snaw*
>
> (*Nordern Lichts: An Anthology of Shetland Verse and Prose* ed. John Graham and T. A. Robertson 1964)

The weather in Perth, home town of William Soutar, was less blustery than in Shetland the night in 1935 when he wrote:

> *And saftly thru the lichted mirk The switherin' snaw cam doun.*

Swithery – full of driven snow.

> *The win' hed driven't it* [snow] *intae swithery nyeukies* [nooks]

> (*Bon Accord* 17 January 1957)

Wreath, wrade – snowdrift. Beware, or you may be the recipient of quite a different kind of wreath.

> *Fan* [when] *the storm abated he was found dead aneath* [beneath] *a muckle wread*

> (*Brechin Advertiser* 13 June 1893)

Yird-drift – snow blown from the ground.

Yowdendrift – snowdrift. The best known use of this word comes from the evocative line of Hugh McDiarmid in 'The Eemis Stane' from his *Sangschaw* collection (1925):

An' my eerie memories fa' Like a yowdendrift.

The lightness of snow is apparent in Douglas Young's *Braird o' Thristles* (1947):

Skinklan pouther frae a licht yowden-drift o' snaw.

Frost

Bobantilter – icicle. A bobantilter can refer to a dangling ornament of any kind and reflects the more decorative aspect of ice.

Cranreuch – hoar frost. This was one of the words that Burns seemed to favour when he wanted to create a sense of suffering in the bitter cold. Perhaps his best-known use of the word is in *To a Mouse*, when his accidental destruction of the mouse's nest leaves the mouse exposed to *the Winter's sleety dribble An cranreuch cauld.*

It is also used figuratively as in:

Full eighty winters thick hae spread
Their cranreughs o'er my palsied head.

(GEORGE BEATTIE *Drama of John o' Arnha* 1816)

Flanders Frost – a frost accompanied by a south-east gale. Christopher Rush in *A Twelvemonth and a Day* (1985) relates:

One year there was a Flanders frost in February. That was the name the old folk gave to a south-east gale that carried a frost as hard as armour – and many of the smaller craft hadn't put to sea for over a week.

Jeel – to freeze; congeal. Sheena Blackhall in *Wittgenstein's Web* (1996) describes

the caller [cold] air that sleepit on Lochnagar,
creepin doon betimes tae jeel the neeps [swedes]
wi the first frosts o autumn.

Johnnie Nip-Nebs – Jack Frost. The apt Scots version translates in to English as Johnnie Nip-Noses.

Rime – hoar frost. It would appear that the autumn of 1808 was relatively mild:

> Nae rime this year amang the corn
> Did mar the kindly reapin morn

(ANDREW SCOTT *Poems*)

Shaela – hoar frost. This Shetland word is sometimes used of things that are frost coloured and so gives its name to the steely grey wool of the native Shetland sheep. It is even used of the sheep themselves whose black or grey wool, tipped with white, gives them a frosted appearance.

Tangle, tankle – icicle. The beauty of a frosty morning is described in a poem by Ebenezer Picken (1813):

> Frae ilka buss, the tangles gay
> Hang skinklin' in the mornin' ray.

However, icicles are not always so cheery. You can feel the depth to which temperatures have plummeted in S. A. Duncan's *Chronicles of Mary Anne* (1945):

It wiz a nicht o' bitter black frost; ootside the
tangles hung a yaird lang.

And you have to empathise with the character in Robert
Ford's *Glints o' Glentoddy* whose
taes were as cauld as tankles.

Thow – thaw:

For three months the snow lay, and then came what
is called a "dirty thow", i.e. the snow melted under
rain, as against disappearing at the command of a
"dry thow" or high wind

(*Banffshire Journal* 19 June 1923)

Thow hole – a term for the south because the wind
generally blows from the south during a thaw;

The mermaids can ought thole [can endure
anything] *But frost out o' the thow hole Auld*
superstitions say.

(JOHN MACTAGGART *The Scottish Gallovidian*
Encyclopedia 1824)

Fortunately for mermaids, frosts from the south are less usual than ones from the north.

Snow and ice might have drawbacks and dangers, but they also have a more pleasurable side. Scotland is not a major destination for winter sports but, in a snowy year, Scottish skiing can be good fun and there are always plenty of challenges for experienced climbers. The Scottish winter sport *par excellence*, however, is curling, a sport of skill and judgement played by sliding a big granite stone up the ice, sweeping its path vigorously and hoping it stays nearest to the centre of some concentric circles. It is usually played on an ice rink, but there are rare occasions when a loch may freeze hard enough for an outdoor curling match (or bonspeil). There can be few more romantic sights than curlers on a frozen loch as the stars begin to appear in the clear, frosty, late afternoon sky and there may even be a chance of seeing the Northern Lights.

3 The Sky

(Clouds, Sun, Moon and Other Heavenly Sights)

The Northern Lights of Old Aberdeen
Mean home sweet home to me.

The skies above Scotland are always changing. We have words to describe clouds from the finest wisp to the louring storm cloud. The appearance of the sun or the moon is a helpful guide as to whether a raincoat is a good idea and, with our frequent showers, we are not short of rainbows.

Clouds

Banff bailies – large, white cumulonimbus.
The large, white snowy-looking clouds that rise
along the horizon . . . were called Banff bailies, and
at all seasons of the year were looked upon as the
forerunners of foul weather.

(Walter Gregor *Notes on the Folk-Lore*
of the North-East of Scotland 1881)

A bailie was originally the baron's deputy in a burgh of barony and it was later used – and in some places still is used – of certain civic dignitaries. So these clouds are, depending on the bailie, quite imposing and stately or a bit puffed up.

Bore hole – a hole in the clouds.

> *Through a bore in the far north, he could see that,*
> *beyond the cloud, the heavens were all a-flame*
> *with the aurora borealis.*
>
> (THOMAS MURRAY *Frae the Heather* 1898)

A blue-bore is a hole in the clouds presaging better
weather to come.

> *All at once a lovely 'blue-bore' fringed with downy*
> *gold opened in the cloud behind, and in five*
> *minutes more . . . all was beauty and serenity.*
>
> (JAMES HOGG *Shepherd's Calendar* 1829)

Cat's hair – fine cirrus.

Cloud, clud, clood – cloud. The last two spellings
show the alternative Scots pronunciations. The *Wisdom
of Solomon* (c.1460) states, rather obviously but in
delightful language,

> *Quhen the cloud slaikis* [lets go its moisture], *the*
> *rane our-strenklys* [over-sprinkles] *the erde* [earth].

Coldingham packmen – cumulus. According to George Henderson in *The Popular Rhymes etc. of the County of Berwick* (1856),

> This name is given to the form of cloud, called
> Cumulus, which appears in vast snowy piles,
> alp over alp, in the north or east, in fine summer
> afternoons. When weaving was a prosperous trade,
> packmen were not unlikely to be frequent about
> Coldingham.

Drumlie – cloudy, gloomy.
> But now thy flowery banks appear
> Like drumlie winter, dark and drear.

(ROBERT BURNS *Logan Water* 1793)

An older and almost onomatopoeic quotation comes from Gavin Douglas in his translation of Virgil's *Aeneid* (1513):

> The feirfull drumly thundris blast.

Goat's hair – fine cirrus.

Hen scarts – hen scratches, i.e. trails of fine cirrus.

Horse-guts – small broken clouds scattered across the sky, a sign of bad weather.

Mirlie – speckled, mottled; when used of the sky, it means flecked with cirrus.

Mirlie-backs – the clouds in a mackerel sky.

Pouthered lawyers – white cumulonimbus, supposedly from a resemblance to lawyers' wigs. These are not associated with good conditions for catching salmon:

> *Ye needna fash yersel the day wi' yer lang wand,*
> *for I wudna gie a pinch o' snuff for a' that ye'll get;*
> *there are too many pouthered lawyrs aboot.*
> (WILLIAM SCROPE *Days and Nights of Salmon Fishing* 1885)

Purse mou – a cloud shaped like the mouth of a

purse. A wind was supposed to come out of the purse mou the next day. Unlike many Scots words, this does not perhaps conjure up a vivid image. The shape referred to could also be described as boat-like.

Roarie bummler – a white cloud formed high in the sky on a windy day, which appears to roar; a bank of storm cloud.

Salmon, saumon – salmon, a long strip of cloud.

Scullgab – a cloud formation resembling a scull or shallow basket, indicating wind direction.

Staff – a bar of cloud across the sun or moon, looked on as a sign of bad weather.

Thirl – a shadow or bar of cloud cutting across the moon or sun, like a hole, considered a sign of bad weather.

Wadder-head – a bank of clouds or cloud-pillars rising from the horizon.

A norwast an' sooth-east wadder head is fir mair weet [for more wet weather]

(JOSEPH GRAY *Lowrie* 1949)

Wadder-mouth – a cloud-formation in which long trails of cloud appear to converge at either end.

Long tails of cloud, wider overhead, and apparently nearing towards the horizon on each side – what Caithness fishermen [call] a 'weather mouth,' is formed

(*Transactions of the Buchan Field Club* 1891)

Sun

Blink – gleam or glimmer of light, especially of sunshine between clouds. Such a watery blink is often 'the blink afore the blatter' – the moment of sunshine before a heavy shower such as is described in the *Analecta Scotica* (1716):

[48]

The sune was shyning on them but the blink was wattery, lyk that befor rain.

A blinkie day is one of alternating sunshine and threatening skies.

Ferrick, fairock – a parhelion or mock sun; a solar halo. A parhelion is a very bright spot on the solar halo, sometimes rainbow-coloured. They tend to appear in pairs, above and below the sun or one at either side. They are not particularly common. As an article in the *Aberdeen Weekly Free Press* (1904) explains:

> *It is somewhat unusual, I think, to see a 'mock sun' on each side of the great orb. When one of these appeared, either before or behind the sun, the old folks spoke of it as a 'fairock.' There was a rhyme about the 'fairock,' which varied with its position in relation to the sun. The een it's afore,* [the one that's in front] *Ye'll hear o' no more, But the een it's ahin* [the one that's behind] *Ye'll shortly fin'.*

The article does not go on to say exactly what you might soon find, but it is safe to assume that it is not good. See **Wadder-biter.**

In Galloway, *ferrick* was used as a term for the solar halo itself.

Gaw, watergaw, weather gaw, weather gall – a partial rainbow, a temporary break in bad weather, a sign of bad weather to come. It is also used figuratively to denote a forlorn hope.

John Veitch in *The History and Poetry of the Scottish Border* (1878) is in no doubt that his watergaw is a partial rainbow:

> *The weather gaw or broken bit of rainbow above the horizon;*

and perhaps the most famous literary reference to a watergaw, which comes from Hugh MacDiarmid (1925), is consistent with this meaning:

*I saw yon antrin thing, A watergaw wi' its chitterin'
licht Ayont the onding*

[I saw that rare thing, a rainbow with its shivering
light beyond the downpour].

However, there are other quotations which seem to
describe something rather different. This one is strangely
reminiscent of a Close Encounter of the Third Kind:

*Four hours before the battle the same spectators
observed (about two in the afternoon) in the sky
three small globes of light, which they took for
what we call (in the north) a weather gall*

(R. FORBES *The Lyon in Mourning* 1748)

A writer in the *Scots Magazine* (May 1823) uses it to
describe a temporary respite in the weather:

*We've a bit blink the day, but you'll find it naething
but a weather-ga',*

and it appears in *Blackwood's Magazine* (1819) as a harbinger of heavy snow:

> *He answered, that he had seen an ill-hued weather-gaw that morning, and was afraid it was going to be a drift.*

Another example of a weather-gaw as a bad sign comes from *The Transactions of The Rymour Club* (1924):

> *Ower Gourlay's Hole the weather-gaw Gleams to warn the boats awa.*

Gleemoch – a faint or deadened gleam, as that of the sun behind fog. The combination of sun and gloom was captured by a writer in the *Scots Magazine* (1821):

> *To . . . shyne like the rouky* [misty] *gleemoch in a craunrochie* [frosty] *morning.*

Gloamin – twilight, dusk.

Simmer-blink – a momentary gleam of sunshine.

Simmer-cloks – the shimmering of sun-beams in the air on a fine summer day.

Simmer-cowt – the quivering motion of the air on a hot day, a heat-haze. Cowt means colt and there is a similar English dialect phrase

the summer colt rides

for the same phenomenon. In Scots, simmer-cowts usually appear in the plural:

The blistering 'simmer coutts,' as we used to call the earth-shimmer.

(*Scots Magazine* July 1943)

As these atoms of the sun (which we commonly call summer colts) do in a sun shine day before or after rain in the heat of summer.

(J. Howie *An Alarm unto a Secure Generation* 1780)

Simmer-dancing – the quivering motion of the air on a hot day, a heat-haze.

[53]

'Simmer dancing' when the heated air is seen
making its way upwards to the higher region of the
atmosphere, with a pretty midge-dance-like motion.
(*Border Treasury* 15 August 1874)

Simmer-dim – the twilight of a summer evening in
Shetland where there is no summer darkness.
The 'simmer dim' – those long, lingering summer
nights when the sun merely sets to rise again at
once.
(WILLIAM MOFFAT *Shetland: The Isles of Nightless Summer* 1934)

Simmer-flaws – the quivering motion of the air on a
hot day, a heat-haze.
'Summer flaws' is a name I've heard the country
folk of Angus give to these shimmering exhalations
that rise from the ground in hot weather.
(*Dundee Courier* 5 June 1965)

Watergaw – see **Gaw.**

Wadder-biter – a mock sun or parhelion, a luminous spot near the sun. See **Ferrick**.

Weather-gleam, wedder-glim, -glaim, -gloom – twilight, a band of clear sky above the horizon often visible at that time.

> *The dowfiest day has aye the sun ayont it, an' the wather-gleam is aye the bonnier for the mornin's rain.*

> (A. J. B. PATERSON *A Mist from Yarrow* 1896)

Moon

Broch – ring round the moon. This is a quite reliable indication that the weather is about to take a turn for the worse. Broch is the same word that is used for the structures, found in Orkney Shetland and the adjacent Scottish mainland, consisting of a round tower with inner and outer walls of stone. In fact, a broch can describe any circle or halo, as in James Stewart's lines from *Sketches of Scottish Character* (1857):

*Wi draps o drink on Saturdays, there's some gets
    roarin fou
There's quarrelin, an crakit croons, an een wi brochs
    o blue.*

Broch can also refer to a circle around the tee in a curling rink (a brocher is a stone between the rings) or a ring drawn on the ground for a children's game of marbles, but its origin is Old English *burh* which gives us the modern word *burgh*, and so we find *broch* in the sense of burgh or town as in Robert Chambers' *Popular Rhymes*, where we learn that *Musselbrogh was a brogh When Edinbrogh was nane.* To anyone from the North-East, however, The Broch means Burghead and Fraserburgh and Walter Gregor's *Folk-Lore of North-East Scotland* (1881) claims that

*Aberdeen will be a green, An Banff a borough's
    toon, But Fraserbroch'ill be a broch When a' the
    brochs is deen.*

Cock's ee – cock's eye, ring around the moon. This highly descriptive term is used in Caithness and Banff for the coloured ring around the moon that warns of storms to come. See also **Broch**.

Fauld – a ring around the moon. This is an Ayrshire word. See also **Broch.**

Muin – moon.

Other Heavenly Sights

Fireflaucht, fyreflacht – lightning.
The beauty and drama of a lightning storm ensure the place of fireflauchts in poetry:

> Fire-flaught and hail, wi' tenfald fury's fires,
> Shall lay yird-laigh [earth-low] Edina's [Edinburgh's]
>   airy spires

(ROBERT FERGUSSON *The Poems of Robert Fergusson* 1773)

Flaucht – flash of lightning (see **Fireflaught**):

The Thunder crakt, and flauchts did rift
Frae the blak Vissart of the Lift.

(ALLAN RAMSAY *Evergreen* 1724)

Northern lichts – *aurora borealis*. These happen when solar winds drive charged particles into the earth's atmosphere, where they are drawn towards the North Pole by the earth's magnetism. They glow in colourful moving bands. The best place to see them in Scotland is Shetland, Orkney and in the very north of the mainland, but they are occasionally visible further south. They reach a peak once every eleven years and we can expect the next good show in 2012–13. There seems to have been a spectacular display in November 2003 according to the *Press and Journal*:

The backgrun o the hills o Royal Deeside ableeze
wi the northern lichts wi the odd flash o lichtnin an
knell o thunner.

Starn, stern – star.

Thunner – thunder:

> *Bot or ve heir the thondir, ve see fyrst the fyir,*
> *quhou be it that thai proceid at ane instant tyme.*
> *The cause that ve see the fyire or ve heir the*
> *thoundir, is be rason that the sycht and cleirnes of*
> *ony thing is mair suyft touart vs nor is the sound.*
> *The euyl that the thondir dois on the eird, it is dune*
> *or ve heir the crak of it*
>
> (Sir David Lindsay *The Complaynte of Scotland* 1549)

[Before we hear the thunder, we see first the fire,
howbeit that they occur at one and the same time.
The cause that we see the fire before we hear the
thunder is by reason that the sight and clearness
of any thing is more swift towards us than is the
sound. The damage that the thunder does on the
earth is done before we hear the crak of it.]

This quotation from Sir David Lindsay was cutting-edge
science for its time since he states that light travels more
swiftly than sound, implying at least that the speed of

light is not infinite. Although this view had been held by some, such as Avicenna, since about 1000CE, it was still a matter for debate and, a century after Lindsay, Descartes was still holding to the opposite view. It was not until 1638 that Galileo suggested ways in which the speed of light might be measured scientifically and the first estimate of the speed of light was made by Ole Rømer in 1676.

Having studied the sky and its portents, it will be all too apparent that the time has come to explore Scots words for wind and storm.

4 *Wind and Storm*

Wind can blaw, souch, or skirl. It can arrive as a flan, a flaw or a gandiegow. A thin wind will cut like a knife. But, as they say, "It is an ill wind that blows nobody good" and as Robert Henryson showed in his narrative poem *The Testament of Cresseid* (1500), there are times when the wind is welcome: *the northin wind had purifyit the air*. There is nothing like a guid blaw or a gandaguster to improve air quality. Even if the wind carries with it rain or sleet and works itself up to a Storm

Force 10, some people, like Burns' Tam o' Shanter, do not seem to mind:

The storm without might rair [roar] *and rustle,*
Tam did na mind the storm a whistle.

For Burns, wind could even have romantic associations:

Of a the airts the wind can blaw,
I dearly like the west,
For there the bonnie lassie lives,
The lassie I lo'e best.

On the other hand, storms can be devastating and some of the words associated with stormy weather, such as *attery* or *gurlie*, have secondary meanings which reflect unpleasant character traits or loss and suffering.

So you just have *to temper your nose to the east win as weel's the south*, or in other words take the rough with the smooth. Scots has words for gentle zephyrs and swirling gales – have a blast reading about them!

Attery – stormy, bitter. Attery literally means poisonous or festering. Applied to people, it means peevish or angry.

Blaffert – blast, buffet. A poignant word picture of an old work horse, lame with stringhalt and spavin is painted by John Caie in *The Kindly North* (1934):

> The orra beastie's cleekit, spavin't, aul', A blaffart o' win' wad ca the cratur totterin'.

Blaw, blaa, blyave, blyauve – blast, gust, blow. The different forms of this word show some of the regional differences in Scots. While blaw is the usual form in West and Central Scotland, *blaa* will be heard more in the East and up the East coast. The North-East is often the home of some distinctive forms and that is where you might hear *blyave* or *blyauve*. It is not only the wind that blaws. A very young bagpiper, being interviewed on TV, was asked for the secret of his success. 'Och, A jist sook and blaw,' he replied.

Blenter, blinter – boisterous wind. The poet

Alexander Douglas (1806) succinctly captured the qualities of the East wind in just a couple of lines:

Now cauld Eurus, snell an' keen,
Blaws loud wi' bitter blenter.

Blouster, bluister, blowster – violent squally wind. Robert Wanlock in *Moorland Rhymes* (1874) takes a pessimistic view of Scottish weather:

There's three months o' bluister tae ilk' ane o' sun.

Orkney suffered a severe storm in 1952 and another, later storm is compared with it in the *Orcadian* (2 November 1995):

. . . the tempest of early Wednesday morning was
a feather in the wind compared to the henhouse-
wrecking blowster of January 1952.

Blowder – sudden gust of wind; exposure to a storm.

Bluffert – a squall; generally conveying the idea of wind and rain. The following quotation describes the construction of haystacks and corn stacks that disappeared with the advent of the combine harvester. The stacks were thatched on top and weighted rope held the thatch secure:

The ruck-tow hauds it sauf an' soon' Fin blowderin' bluffert jeels, O.

[The stack-rope holds it safe and sound when gusty squall chills, O.]

(R. L. CASSIE *Banffshire Journal* 21 April 1931)

Borrowing days – the last three days of March; the storm associated with that time. We find March winds referred to in this way in the sixteenth-century *The Complaynte of Scotland* by Sir David Lindsay: *The borial blastis of the thre borouing dais of marche.*

A seventeenth-century storm is recorded in a Justiciary Court case (1629):

As that nycht that the grit storme arraise commonlie callit the borrowing dayis.

[65]

Eggle – to worsen, to threaten to become stormy. A 1930 quotation from Orkney demonstrates the sense:

Hid's egglan ap i' the east; we'll hae war wather.

Fairies' ween – a swirl or eddy of wind raising dust on a road as if some unseen traveller were passing along.

Flaff – to blow in gusts.

An' syne fan he [the wind] *wad oxter you* [hustle you as if by the arm (oxter literally means 'armpit')], *An' flaf, an' howl, an' rair* [roar]

(James Davidson *Poems* 1861)

Flan – gust of wind, especially one blowing smoke down a chimney, back draught; squall. As the following quotations show, flans are not good for housewives, sailors or gardeners.

A flan cam doon the lum an' blew
The ase a' ben the fleer

[The ash all inwards onto the floor]

(*Banffshire Journal* 25 February 1879).

Also tho the Wind be not so strong, there will come Flans and Blasts off the Land as to their swiftness and surprisal something like to Hurricanes.

(JOHN BRAND *A Brief Description of Orkney, Zetland, Pightland-Firth & Caithness* 1701)

The side of the boat was laid under water by a flan off Bressey Head.

(JOHN MILL *Diary of the Rev. John Mill, 1740–1803*)

A Flann of rancid Dung steam will destroy a whole crop of those early Cucumber plants.

(JAMES JUSTICE *Scots Gardiner* 1754)

$Flaw$ – blast or squall of wind. This vivid simile by Sir Walter Scott in *The Antiquary* (1816) really shows what the untranslatable word *skirling* means. It is the noise people make in great distress or anger and it is the sound of the bagpipes, but if you really want to get to grips with it, you need to go bird-watching in winter:

> *Skirling like an auld skart* [cormorant] *before a flaw o' weather.*

Gandaguster, gandiegow – strong, sudden gust of wind, a sweeping wind; a storm, especially one of short duration.

Gonial Blast – the name of a particular storm. In the *Transactions of the Hawick Archaeological Society* of 1873, there is an account of a great storm known as the 'Goniel Blast', a name derived from the number of sheep that died as a result of the storm. A gonial is a sheep that is found dead and much decayed. The ancient established custom in the Cheviot district dictates that, if the carcase hangs together when held up by the hind legs and shaken vigorously, then it belongs to the farmer, but, if it falls to pieces, it is a perquisite of the shepherd.

Granny – chimney cowl. These metal shelters over chimney pots prevented the occasional flan of wind from blowing smoke down the chimney and into the room. So the observation in *The Looker-on*, by Neil Munro (1930) does not require the attendance of the emergency services:

> *There's a 'granny' on a lum* [chimney] *up there*
> *that's jist hingin' by a wire.*

Gurlie – stormy, threatening, blustery, bleak, bitter. Allan Ramsay (1721) writes:

> *Bare Fields and gurly Skies Make rural Scenes*
> *ungrateful to the Eyes.*

In the *Ballad of Sir Patrick Spens*, we know that the outcome must be tragic as soon as we read the lines:

> *When the lift grew dark, and the wind blew loud,*
> *And gurly grew the sea.*

A similar sense of foreboding is engendered by this

quotation from George Macdonald's *Castle Warlock* (1882):

> *It's a gurly nicht; no a pinch o' licht, an' the win'*
> *blawin' like deevils.*

This threatening word transfers easily to snarling dogs and bad-tempered people:

> *Dour were their threats and their grimaces, Gurlie*
> *and crabbit-like their faces.*
>
> (WILLIAM TENNANT *Papistry Storm'd* 1827)

Haar – a cold, easterly wind; a gentle easterly breeze; a sea mist. This very useful word is technically well explained in these quotations:

> *In the months of April and May, easterly winds,*
> *commonly called Haars, usually blow with great*
> *violence, especially in the afternoons.*
>
> (WILLIAM NIMMO *A General History of Stirlingshire* 1777)

> *The easterly har, a sea breeze so called by*
> *fishermen, which in the Moray Frith during the*

summer months and first month of autumn,
commonly comes on after ten o'clock a.m. and fails
at four o'clock p.m. had now set in.

(HUGH MILLER *Letters on the Herring Fishery* 1829)

The haar, however, does not extend itself a great
way into the country, for, by the time it has reached
the distance of perhaps twenty or thirty miles from
the shore, it is generally dissipated by the greater
heat of the interior land.

(JAMES GRIERSON *Delineations of St Andrews* 1807)

[The North Sea] *being five degrees warmer in*
summer, than the Atlantic, a copious evaporation
takes place, throughout its extent, which produces
the eastern haars (as they are called) or thick mists,
which are seen, at a certain period of the day, to
arise from the sea.

(JOHN SINCLAIR *General Report of the Agricultural State and*
Political Circumstances of Scotland 1814)

However, none of the above quite gives the sense of chill with which even a summer haar can penetrate to your marrow. Add to this the smoky pollution of Edinburgh chimneys, which gave Edinburgh its nickname of 'Auld Reekie' in the nineteenth century, and it is easy to sympathise with John Wilson (Christopher North) in *Noctes Ambrosianae* (1827):

> *But it's just your ain vile, vapoury, thick, dull,*
> *yellow, brown,. . . easterly haur o' Embro' that gies*
> *me the rheumatics.*

Haar is more poetically described by Gilbert Rae in *'Tween Clyde and Tweed* (1919):

> *Within a martyr's grave, Ower whilk the white haur*
> *dreeps.*

Hairiken, heerican, hurricane – hurricane.

Lown – calm, still. John Bellenden in *The Chronicles of Scotland*, compiled by Hector Boece (1531), describes the perfect start to a day:

The nixt day . . . the lift [sky] *appering lowyn, but ony dyn or tempest . . .*

John Reid in his amazingly titled book, *The Scots Gard'ner, in two parts; with Appendix shewing how to use the friut of the garden; whereto is annexed the Gard'ners Kalendar. Published for the climate of Scotland* (1683), gives the following essential advice on growing melons:

Acquaint them a little with the air by raising the edg of the glasses with a little straw on the lown side, closing it at night again.

Muckle Forester – wind.

The *Muckle Forester*, literally the 'Great Forester', is an alternative name for the destructive wind that fells trees:

I min the muckle forester throwin an aik [oak] *athwart* [across] *the road, an didna that caa* [knock] *plans an time an time-tables aa tae crocinition* [confusion]?

(*Bulletin* 21 May 1951)

Pirl – eddy or swirl in air, a ripple, a faint breeze. Many words to do with wind are onomatopoeic. This word sounds so very soft and gentle. The wind that had rippled this pool was no more than a breath:

The sun was shinin bright, the wind was lown, an' wi' the pirl being away, the pool was as clear as crystal.

(*Blackwood's Magazine* April 1817)

And this is what we call a saft day:

There was a fine pirl out frae the West, wi' a sma' smurr o' rain.

(HEW AINSLIE *A Pilgrimage to the Land of Burns* 1822)

Pirr – a gentle breath of wind; a not-so-gentle breath of wind. This word highlights one of the difficulties that lexicographers face. We define words according to the way people use them. Taking as many quotations as possible, we look carefully at all the ways words are used and we try to deduce what people understand by them. This is not always straightforward. Words may have more than one meaning and meanings change over the years.

The sense of a caressing zephyr is evident in the words of Thomas Manson in *Humours of a Peat Commission* (1894):

A gentle 'pir' of wind to keep the heat from becoming oppressive.

However, this contrasting quotation from the *Fife Herald* of August 1831 seems to suggest a less welcome current of air:

And were they [corn fields] to be visited with a pirr of wind,. . . the result would be seriously felt.

Another agriculture voice from the *Buchan Observer* (November 1954) confirms a stronger November blast:

A gey pirrie o' win' an flans o' shooers skilpin roon wir lugs [our ears] at 'e plooin [ploughing].

The Shetland writer J. J. Haldane Burgess provides

an emotive, figurative usage in his 1891 collection of poems, *Rasmie's Büddie*:

> As da pirr o memry, blaain [blowing], Frae mi een
> [eyes] da skub [mist] aa clears.

Rumballiach – tempestuous, stormy. This vigorous word can be used of either weather or temperament.

Scudder – a driving shower of rain or snow, to rain in a windy blast. According to the *Huntly Express, some gey caul' scudders* were experienced in July of 1949 and no one wants to encounter

> A scudderin'-dudderin' wund blawin' doon the
> street.

> (*Scots Magazine* July 1897)

Simmer-haar – a slight breeze from the east, which often rises after the sun has passed the meridian. This localised expression appears to have been used by Newhaven fishermen.

Snell – keen, bitter, sharp, severe. This adjective is very commonly associated with the wind, in this case with unattractive consequences:

> *Ma neb is blae* [My nose is blue]; *the wund is snell.*
>
> (GEORGE CAMPBELL HAY 1979 in *Chapman* ed.
> Joy Hendry 1985)

It can, however, be used of other cutting weather such as the *Haylstanys bath scharpe and snelle* described by Androw of Wyntoun in *The Orygynale Cronykil of Scotland* (1420). Another early example comes from Gavin Douglas's translation of the Aeneid (1513):

> *Chyvirrand* [shivering] *for cald, the sesson was so snell.*

Souch – a sound like that of the wind, the wind itself, a draught. The *ou* is pronounced as *oo* and the *ch* is pronounced as it is in *loch*. Even if the word is spelt differently – and it clearly shows that Scots spelling is very variable – it retains this pronunciation. Some of these spellings, as well as senses are illustrated in these quotations:

Cauld blaws the nippin north wi' angry sough

(ROBERT FERGUSSON *Poems* 1773)

The wind was back a bit and a strong seuch
coming up from the south

(NAOMI MITCHISON & DENIS MACINTOSH *Men and Herring* 1949)

November chill blaws loud wi angry sugh

(ROBERT BURNS *The Cotter's Saturday Night* 1785)

Ye're clear o' the soogh o' the door there.

(ALEXANDER HISLOP *The Book of Scottish Anecdote* 1876)

If you keep, haud, ca' or mak a calm, quiet, sober or lown souch then you keep quiet or hold your tongue. Keeping a calm souch also means remaining unperturbed. By contrast to *raise yer souch* means to speak out or make a pronouncement. If you mutter something *within yer ain souch* it is said under your breath or *sotto voce*.

A highly descriptive use as a verb appears in John Buchan's *Poems, Scots and English* from 1917:

> The fiddles scrapit and atower the din
> The 'Floo'ers o' Embro'' soughed out on the win'.

Storm – storm.

Swither – swirl; gust. This is a rather confusing word in Scots. In fact, there are several homonyms, not all related in origin. The word exemplified by William Thom in *Rhymes and Recollections of a Handloom Weaver* (1845) – *As the storm would swither and swell* – is related to the swirl of snow also listed in the chapter on **Snow and Frost**. Yet another *swither* is a very useful verb for when one is unable to make up one's mind, and then one swithers.

Weatherie – stormy, wet and windy.

Wedderly, weatherly – (of a boat) able to stand to the wind.

Weddircock, weathercock – weathercock. This very public aid to meteorology, according to *Linlithgow Burgh Records*, in 1629, cost *Tenn pundis for wpputting of the weddercok on the steipill heid.*

The inconstant bird provided a nickname for swithering bishops:

Some call the bishops weather cocks,
Who where their heads were, turn their docks;

(Samuel Colvil *The Whigs Supplication, or,*
The Scots Hudibras 1681)

Wind – many instances of structural damage caused by high winds are documented in the records of town councils, churches and so on. One such from the *Chronicles of Perth* tells us that in 1608 *The great wind blew down the stanes of the mantil wall of the kirk.* In literature, there are many figurative references to wind, including *This wikkit wind of adulatioun* in Robert Henryson's *Fables* (1500).

An *ill* [evil] wind is frequently attributed to witchcraft. In 1650, Brechin Presbytery brought

Presumptiones of witchcraft against Catharin Lyall . . .
[she] straik [struck] the horse on the hinder fillets
with a weight . . . ther cam by a stranger woman
and said the horse has gotten a blast of ill wind,
and when his skin shall be taken off it would have a
black spott quher [where] he had gotten the stroke.

Sometimes the spell was misdirected, according to *Perth Kirk Sessions* (1623). A complainer reports that

Hir sister wes seik by the dint of ane ill wynd,
quhilk wes prepairit nocht for hir bot for hir maister.

The intervention of witches could be of benefit. Sir John Lauder of Fountainhall, in his *Historical Observes of Memorable Occurrents in Church and State* (1685), reports that

The wind Argile got from Holland . . . was so
favorable that it brought him in a very few dayes
to Orknay . . . which made some think his witches
had sold him a wind but he hes got no good wind
to carry him away.

The duty of a landlord to keep a building *wind and watertight* is still often written into leases in Scotland, although it is no longer common in England. This phrase has a long history:

> *The said tour fortalice* [tower fortress] *was than windticht and waterticht sufficiently sklaittit and ruiffit* [slated and roofed] *with timber and sklait*
>
> (*The Book of the Thanes of Cawdor* 1635)

Wind craw – wind crow, a child's toy for windy days. A large potato is stuck full of wing-feathers of a gull or other large bird and thrown outside when the wind is blowing hard. It will be driven before the breeze with great speed, and it needs a fast and agile runner to catch it. Increased use of potatoes for this purpose could render the couch potato extinct.

Windfeed(er) – a shower of rain which is followed by an increase of wind.

Whirlwind – whirlwinds seem to have been frequently

attributed to witchcraft in earlier times. James VI of Scotland (and, from 1603, James I of England) was an authority on witches. A letter of 1590 included in *Letters from James VI of Scotland and Chancellor Maitland to Robert Bruce, Minister of the Gospel* notes that

> In deadest calmes . . . perellous puftes and
> quhirlwindes will aryse.

More specifically, the Justiciary Court Records of 1662 put it to the accused that

> She . . . raised a whirlwind and thereby had carried
> away Robert Lauder's house.

The Beaufort Scale

If we arrange Scots winds according to the Beaufort Scale (a system devised by Admiral Francis Beaufort and still used in a slightly modified form by the Royal Navy) we may get some idea of the best word to use for any particular wind. However, the way the words are used by Scots speakers may cover a range of meanings and – bearing in mind the Scots propensity for understatement – a bit o a blaw might well mean a Force 12! A description of each wind is given in Scots and English.

Force 0 – lown

Lown. Reek gangs stracht up.
[Calm. Smoke rises vertically.]

Force 1 – pirl, fairies' ween

Licht air. Wind motion visible in reek.
[Light air. Wind motion visible in smoke.]

Force 2 – pirl, pirr

Licht breeze. Leaves reesle.
[Light breeze. Leaves rustle.]

Force 3 – pirr, haar

Douce breeze. Leaves an twigs aye steerin.

[Gentle breeze. Leaves and smaller twigs in constant motion.]

Force 4 – a bit o a souch

Canny breeze. Stour raised. Sma branches stert tae muive.
[Moderate breeze. Dust raised. Small branches begin to move.]

Force 5 – a richt souch

Steerie breeze. Sma trees swey.
[Fresh breeze Small trees sway.]

Force 6 – blaa, blaw, an affae souch

Strang breeze. Muckle branches steerin. Dirlin in owerheid wires.
[Strong breeze. Large branches in motion. Whistling in overhead wires.]

Force 7 – blaffert

Near gale. Hale trees steerin. Effort needit tae warsle agin the blafferts.
[Near gale. Whole trees in motion. Effort needed to walk against the wind.]

Force 8 – blouster

Gale. Twigs cawed aff trees.
[Gale. Twigs broken from trees.]

Force 9 – muckle blouster, blenter, blinter

Severe gale. Lums an sklaits taen aff.
[Severe gale. Chimneys and slates taken off.]

Force 10 – byornar blenter, blinter

Storm. Trees blawn doon. A hantle o skaith tae biggins.
[Storm. Trees uprooted. Considerable structural damage.]

Force 11 –gandaguster, gandiegow, (The Muckle Forester)

Severe storm. Unco heich jaws. Muckle skaith tae biggins.
[Unusually high waves. Widespread structural damage.]

Force 12 –hurricane, hairiken, heerican

Hurricane. Big, muckle jaws. Air fair fu o faem an spindrift.
[Hurricane. Huge waves. Air filled with foam and spray.]

Although the Scottish weather is notoriously changeable, the Force 10s, 11s and 12s are more frequent from November to March and although it has been known to snow in June, such events are rare. So, while still expecting the unexpected, we divide our year into seasons based on the cycle of nature.

5 The Seasons

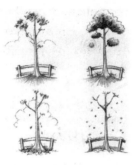

*It was a cycle without end; voar, summer, hairst
and winter, on and on, life and birth, death and
rebirth*

(ROBERT ALAN JAMIESON *Thin Wealth* 1986)

The official dates of seasons, which relate to the equinoxes and solstices, do not always have much bearing on the weathers associated with the individual seasons. Therefore, in conversation, in literature and in local conventions there may be some variation and flexibility and winter or spring may come early or late in the popular imagination, depending on the weather more than the calendar. Unlike other chapters in this book, the ordering here is roughly chronological rather than strictly alphabetical.

Spring

Buchan's cold spell – one of a series of spells of cold weather occurring approximately at the same time each year, according to a theory based on weather statistics put forward by Alexander Buchan (1827–1907) of Kinnesswood, Kinross-shire, in 1867. These cold spells are 7–14 February, 11–14 April, 29 June–14 July, 6–11 August and 6–13 November.

Lentren – spring. A season of uncertain weather: Hugh Miller in *Scenes and Legends of the North of Scotland* (1832) describes one season when:

> *The burns were rinnin' big wi' spate, Lentron win's blew gurly and snell.*

Voar – spring. This word comes from Old Norse *vár* and is used in Orkney and Shetland.

Ware – spring. Like the word *voar* found in the Northern Isles, *ware* also comes from Old Norse *vár*, but it is mainly used in the South-West of Scotland. The ware-quarter ran from February to April and so, at the beginning of ware, even in the south of Scotland, there was little relief from the harshness of winter. Hence we have the proverb recorded in James Kelly's *Collection of Scottish Proverbs* (1721):

> *The Ware Evening is long and tough, The Harvest Evening runs soon o'er the Heugh* [crag].

Ware-day was the first day of spring but *lang-ware-day* was the term for a period of dearth in March.

Wairie – cold, hard, bleak, unproductive.

Lang reid – the period of poverty in late winter or early spring when most of the winter stocks were consumed. This term apparently comes from Old Norse *langa-hríð*, literally a long snowstorm, spell of bad weather or suffering.

Saint Causlan's flaw – a snowstorm in March. *Notes and Queries* of 1850 records that this expression was used in Angus, in which is situated the parish church of Dunnichen, dedicated to St Causlan (Constantine), whose festival was held in March.

Pace – Easter. Pace, pasch or pask, to give only a few of its many spellings, is the traditional word for Easter – a comparatively recent term in Scotland. It derives from Latin *pascha* which also gave rise to French *pasche*, *pasque* and Old Danish *paska*, further possible influences on Scots. For anyone who has difficulty in calculating the date of Easter, help is at hand; Helen Beaton in *At the Back o' Benachie* (1915) explains:

First comes Candlemas, an' then the new meen,
The first Tuesday efter that is aye Fastern's Een,
That meen oot an' the neist meen's hicht,
An the first Sunday efter that is aye Pess richt.

Some families still roll Easter-eggs, come sun, rain, sleet or hail. David Mitchell's *History of Montrose* (1866) tells us that

At Pasch the Burneses had always the best dyed eggs to throw in the Links.

The *Aberdeen People's Journal* (12 April 1958) recalls:

We eest tae gaither the flooers tae colour oor pess eggs.

Gorse flowers turn even the most peelie-wallie eggs a rich, warm brown. Surprisingly, the tradition seemed under threat as early as 1937 when, according to Mary Banks' *British Calendar Customs*,

> *Though the custom of rolling 'paiss' eggs still holds in Bervie, it is slowly, I think, dying out. In the olden times, however, it was carefully kept and the eggs were rolled on the 'paiss braes' – a name they still bear – situated up the haughs near Crookity.*

John Calder in *Sketches from John o' Groats* (1842) tells us that

> *The poor, who had no poultry of their own, went round among their neighbours a day or two before, collecting what they called their 'peace eggs',*

but the *New Shetlander* of March-April 1949 refers to

> *The now almost vanished custom of gjaa'n [going] paes-eggin.*

Summer

Simmer – summer.

Dae ye mind on lang, lang syne
When the simmer days were fine?

Memory makes the summers of long ago warmer and sunnier and the glories of summers gone by are recorded in early Scots literature: *Cum, somer, cum, the suete sesoun and sonne!* King James I of Scotland around 1409 hails the summer in his poem the *Kingis Quair*. Gavin Douglas in the Prologue to his *Aeneid* (1513) rejoices in *Cleir schynand bemys, and goldyn symmyris hew*. For some churchgoers, however, summer had its disadvantages; Charles Rogers in his *Social Life in Scotland* records how the Kirk Session of Dundonald in 1642 determined that

> *no women be suffered to sit in the time of sommer*
> *with plyds* [shawls] *upon their heids since it is a*
> *cleuck* [ensnarement] *to their sleiping in tyme of*
> *sermon.*

They could sleep snugly through a winter sermon, though.

Simmermal – the first day of summer, popularly

considered to be 14 April (Shetland Dialect). The weather on Simmermal Day is said to be the forecast of the weather all summer.

Gowk's storm – a storm of short duration, occurring in mid-April. The earlier quotations for this word seem to focus on the short duration of the storm, often using the term figuratively to refer to a transient situation:

> *An intercepted letter . . . in which Huntly (in 1594) spoke of the King's rumoured campaign as likely to turn out a gowk's storm*
>
> (PATRICK TYTLER *The History of Scotland* 1864)

> *Bragging . . . that this tempest wil not continew, and that it will pruif but a gowk storm (for thir be the wordis . . . that thai commonlie vse)*
>
> (*Original Letters relating to the Ecclesiastical Affairs of Scotland* ed. David Laing 1609)

However the later evidence makes it quite clear that the gowk's storm referred to particular seasonal conditions:

*This district is subject, in the spring season, to
a succession of storms called . . . the borrowing
days, the Toochet's storm, the Gouk's storm (the
equinoxial), and the gab of May*

(*New Statistical Account (Moray)* 1845)

*In Scotland . . . the advent of the cuckoo calls forth
the old season's spite, and the consequence is 'a
gowk storm.'*

(James Napier *Folk Lore: or Superstitious
Beliefs in the West of Scotland* 1879)

*The first [of the three cold snaps of spring or early
summer] is the 'Gowk's Storm' (from the 11th till
the 14th of April), when the cuckoo has just come.
This the English call the 'Borrowing Days.'*

(*Times* 13 May 1930)

Teuchat's storm – a storm associated with the
return of lapwings.

Coo-quake – (cow-quake) a short spell of cold weather occurring in May (as opposed to the expected cold spell in April, June, July or any other month). See also **Yow-trummle**.

> *Come it aire, come it late, in May comes the cowquake*
>
> (DAVID FERGUSSON *Scottish Proverbs* 1598)

Gab o Mey – another cold spell in May.

> *The weather doesn't really turn until after the Gab o' May, the last snow storm that sweeps across the hills in the middle of May killing newborn lambs, nesting birds and the first spring flowers; a Calvinistic reminder that we shouldn't relax until the end of May*
>
> (*Sunday Herald* 28 March 1999)

> *. . . here in North-East Scotland we are well aware of the 'Gab o' May', when snow showers are to be expected around May 8*
>
> (*Times* 23 May 2003)

Yow-trummle – a cold spell in early summer about the time of sheep-shearing, supposed to chill the sheep.

> *Ae weet forenicht i' the yow-trummle I saw yon antrin* [rare] *thing*

(HUGH MCDIARMID *Sangschaw* 1925)

St Bullion's Day, St Martin of Bullion's Day – falling on 15 July, this is also known as St Swithin's Day and carries the same traditional associations with weather prognostication. Aberdeenshire has its own variations on the name of the saint.

> *St. Martin's day was known on Donside as 'Martin Bulg's Day'; in the Buchan district of Aberdeenshire it is called 'Marcabillin's Day'.*

(SIR WALTER SCOTT *The Antiquary* 1898)

Autumn

Backen – [back end] another name for autumn. ...astination is the thief of time, as this observation in

[98]

John MacTaggart's *The Scottish Gallovidian Encyclopedia* (1824) confirms:

> Many a farmer leaves pieces of work in spring
> and the summer to be done in the backen; but
> when that period arrives, they are still left undone,
> perhaps to the next waurtime [springtime].

Hairst, hervest – harvest, autumn. A speaker from Crieff in 1955 made a clear distinction in the use of *hairst* and *hervest*. This usage may not still be current:

> Here in Crieff 'hairst' is used for the grain harvest.
> 'Hervest' is used for fruit harvest. People say "you
> have a grand apple hervest this year" (they would
> never say "apple hairst").

Hairst Monday – the Monday occurring about four weeks before the anticipated commencement of the harvest, the occasion of a hiring market for harvest labour.

Cauld winter – the last load of corn brought in from the field to the barnyard at the end of the harvest.

The gab o winter – a spell of cold weather in early autumn.

Goesomer, go o simmer, St Martin's summer – a period of summer-like weather occurring in late autumn.

Tattie holidays – a school holiday during October when children traditionally helped with the potato harvest.

Laidner – a winter's stock of provisions, an ox or cow slaughtered and cured for winter food. The traditional slaughtering time was between Michaelmas and Martinmas.

Winter

Winter Saturday – the last Saturday in October, ~~n~~ the winter half of the year is considered to begin.

For some, the winter was a time of privation and suffering. The inhabitants of Fair Isle, however, made the most of it. *The Scots Magazine* (August 1931) tells us:

> *Wintertime is the islanders' time for enjoyment. 'Lifts' or parties are held in the different crofts, the name 'lift' no doubt meaning the time when the crops are gathered in and safely stored away for the winter.*

Halloween – All-Hallows Eve, 31 October. In the nineteenth century, Walter Gregor tells us in *Notes on the Folk-Lore of the North-East of Scotland* (1881):

> *During the burning of the [Halloween] fire and the scattering of the ashes, the half-yearly servants on the farm, if they intended changing masters, sang: – This is Hallaeven, The morn is Halladay; Nine free nichts till Martinmas, As soon they'll wear away.*

Halloween is a favourite time for children, but in Scotland their traditional activities are guising (rather than trick-or-treating), and a sensible householder will demand a song, a poem or a joke before nuts, fruit, sweets or money are handed over. The guisers carry a turnip lantern (made from a large swede) and at a Halloween party they will expect to take part in games like dookin [ducking] for aipples and eating treacle scones suspended above their heads (to be tackled with hands behind the back).

Martinmas – the feast of St Martin, 11 November. Martinmas is one of the legal annual term-days, the other being Whitsunday. Formerly it was one of the days for the hiring of servants. The Martinmas term is the autumn term of the academic year at the Universities of St Andrews and Glasgow.

The Daft Days – Yule, New Year and Handsel Monday. A. Balfour in *The Farmers' Three Daughters* (1822) tells us:

> 'The Daft Days'. . . were set apart for the meeting of
> friends and intimate neighbours, to dine or
> ⌐ (often both) together, when good cheer,

home-brewed, and hearty welcome, promoted
the conviviality and rustic mirth of the
company.

For Sir Walter Scott, they were a time for tales of derring-do. He writes in *Rob Roy* (1818) of

venturesome deeds and escapes, sic as folk tell
ower at a winter-ingle in the daft days.

Ushering in this festive period, the fourth Sunday of advent is Bonny Sunday, also known as Beainer-Sunday, or Ben(n)a-Sunday. These names, deriving from Old Norse and Old English, mean 'Prayer-Sunday'. On this day, according to Thomas Edmonston in *An Etymological Glossary of the Shetland and Orkney Dialect* (1866), you hung up more than just your stocking at the fireplace. He describes Beainer-Sunday as

the Sunday before Christmas, on which day it was
usual to hang up an ox-head in the chimney, to
make broth with.

An earlier reference to the day comes from 1774, when G. Low asserts in *A Tour through the Islands of Orkney and Shetland* that

> *Their Festivals are Christmas, Newyearsday,...*
> *Bonny Sunday, ...*

A more recent quotation, from 1935, seems to suggest that by then the term was already dying out; when a Shetland informant told the editors of the *Scottish National Dictionary*:

> *I have frequently heard the remark from some old person: "Folk, what tink ye, dis is Benna Sunday".*

If an old person has to draw people's attention to a day that was once a major festival, we must suppose that the day was no longer celebrated as such.

Yule – Christmas and the festive season associated with it.

Hogmanay – New Year's Eve. Traditionally, this was more enthusiastically celebrated in Scotland than Christmas, but Christmas is now a much more elaborate festival here than it once was. Still, Hogmanay is a high point of the year. No tasks should be left undone. The door may be opened to let the old year out and the New Year in. First-footing is still an important ritual. One hopes that the first person to step over one's threshold after the clock strikes midnight will be tall and dark. Traditionally they might have brought salt or coal, representing prosperity for the coming year – and they should certainly not come empty-handed. While Burns' *Auld Lang Syne* may be sung to see the old year out, a fitting song for bringing the New Year in is:

A Guid New Year tae ane an aw
And mony may ye see
And durin aw the years tae come
Happy may ye be.
An may ye nee'er hae cause tae murn,
Tae sigh or shed a tear.

Tae ane an aw, baith great an sma,
A hertie, Guid New Year!

We can't see what is in our personal future as we look forward into a new year and make good resolutions. As Robert Burns says in *To a Mouse*,

The best laid schemes o' mice an' men Gang aft a-gley.

But we can look into the future and predict the weather. Here's how!

6 Forecasting the Weather

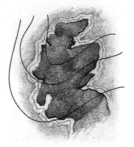

However much we value the weather forecasts that we get from the expert meteorologists, they can hardly be expected to give forecasts for every hill and glen, many of which create their own microclimates. The professional weather forecasters in some respects may be compared with newspaper astrologers who have to deal in generalities to please some of the people some of the time. Forecasts, however, can be enhanced by observation of local signs and by paying attention to elderly gentlemen who hold up licked thumbs and make pronouncements about rain.

Banff bailies – these cumulonimbus clouds are forerunners of foul weather.

A *Blue-bore* – or hole in the clouds is a good sign, especially if there is 'enough blue sky for a sailor's waistcoat'.

A *Broch* – (also known as a cock's eye) around the moon is a sign of stormy weather, and the further out the broch is from the moon, the closer the storm:

The further the broch, the nearer the rauch.
A broch aboot the muinn 'ill be aboot the midden aforce mornin.

...t the bar – is the noise of the waves on

[108]

the pebbly beach along the Banff coast (chap. here, means knock). If the noise comes from the east in winter, expect frost. If the sound comes from the west, a thaw is on its way. (On a coastline that runs east–west, this is not entirely surprising since an east wind carrying the sound is blowing from Siberia, but a west wind is a warmer one off the Gulf Stream.)

An *Eame* or *ime* – is defined in the *John o' Groat Journal* (9 January 1920) as

> *the damp sea winds condensing on the window pane, moisture condensing on walls after extreme frost, even the damp in the atmosphere, particularly associated with sea-brine, or the condensation on the stones left by the receding tide*

and a later issue (26 January 1940) tells the would-be meteorologist that

> *An eame of frost . . . In old weather lore this rising vapour was a sure sign of an 'ooterly'* [far out at sea] *gale.*

A *Gaw* – could be a sign of trouble.

> *He answered, that he had seen an ill-hued weather-gaw that morning, and was afraid it was going to be a drift*
>
> (*Blackwood's Magazine* April 1819)

> *Ower Gourlay's Hole the weather-gaw Gleams to warn the boats awa*
>
> (*Rymour Club Miscellany* III 1924)

Hen scarts and *filly tails* – in the traditional rhyme, these *make lofty ships wear Pow sails*. Robert Chambers explains in *Popular Rhymes* (1847) that

> *Certain light kinds of clouds are thus denominated, from their supposed resemblances to the scratches of hens on the ground and the tails of young mares. They are held as prognosticative of stormy weather.*

ther traditional version is:

> s' tails and mackerel scales mak tall ships tak
>
> ils.

Salmon – according to the *Edinburgh New Philosophical Journal* of 1863 XVIII, *salmon* has an interesting additional meaning:

> *The farmers in Berwickshire say that a long stripe of cloud sometimes called by them a salmon, sometimes called* **Noah's ark***, when it stretches through the atmosphere in an east and west direction is a sign of stormy weather, but when it stretches in a north and south direction, is a sign of dry weather.*

Mist – the various places where mist appears, the thickness of the vapour and the time of day can all be brought to bear for weather forecasting

> *Mist on the hills, weather spills; Mist in the howes* [hollows]*, weather grows*
>
> (Traditional)

> *Thick* **rouk** [mist] *in the morning, thairafter warme and fair*
>
> (ANDREW HAY *The Diary of Andrew Hay of Craignethan* 1659)

I minded an old saying of Tam Todd's, "Rouk's
snaw's wraith," and I looked for a wild storm with
gladness.

(John Buchan *John Burnet of Barns* 1898)

The **Moon's** appearance is a rich source of weather
lore:

When the muin is on her back, Mend yer shuin and
sort yer thack!

(Traditional)

The famous reference to the moon and approaching
storm is in the *Ballad of Sir Patrick Spens*:

I saw the new muin late yestreen
Wi the auld muin in her airm
And if we gang tae sea maister
I fear we'll come tae hairm.

Smoke – a traditional rhyme states:

When the smoke gaes west,
Guid weather is past;

When the smoke gaes east,
Guid weather comes neist.

A *Staff or Thirl* – (a bar of cloud) across the moon, this is a bad sign.

Wind – presages wet weather:
After a wind there commes a weit
(JAMES CARMICHAEL *Collection of Proverbs* 1628)

Birds, Animals and Plants

These often anticipate changes in the weather. Bird signs of bad weather include **seagulls** on land, **owls** hunting by day and **swallows** flying low.

According to the *Buchan Observer* of 22 August 1950, **ants** are worth watching:
An emerteen's byke [an ants' nest] *... is aften in a great commotion; but the wee beasties ken to keep a soun' reef abeen their heids*

[a sound roof above their heads]

if there's ony signs o' rain.

Geese *tae the sea,*
guid weather tae be;
Geese tae the hill,
guid weather tae spill

(Traditional)

If the **deer** rise dry and lie down dry on St Martin of Bullion Day (4 July), it was a sign there would be a good gose-harvest. The go-harvest or gose-harvest is late autumn, the period of the year between harvest-time and the beginning of winter.

Snailie, *snailie, shoot oot yer horn, And tell us if it'll be a bonny day the morn*

(Traditional)

If there are a lot of berries on the **hawthorn bushes**, expect a hard winter:

Mony **haws**, *mony snaws* (Traditional).

In this well-known saying, the **mey** refers to the **may** or **hawthorn blossom**: in spring

Ne'er cast a clout till mey be oot.

It makes a lot of sense to be sure that the **cow-quake** and the **gowk's storm** are also over before removing your winter clothing. The first of these is a spell of bad weather that chills the cattle newly turned out on spring pasture and the arrival of the gowk or cuckoo is often coincidental with a short, sharp storm in late April or early May.

If the **oak** *comes out before the* **ash**, *the summer it*
will be a splash.
If the ash comes out before the oak, the summer it
will be a soak.

This pair of sayings caused me some confusion as a child. I anxiously scanned oak and ash buds to see whether summer would be accompanied by splashing rain or soaking rain. I have since been informed that 'splash' refers to sunshine. I remain unconvinced.

Feasts and Forecasts

Superstitions regarding weather also attach to certain dates and saints' days or holidays.

> *If **Candlemas day** be clear and fair,*
> *The half o' winter's tae gang and mair;*
> *If Candlemas day be dark and foul,*
> *The half o' the winter is duin at Yule.*

> *If **Candlemas day** is bright and clear,*
> *There'll be twa winters in the year.*

St Martin of Bullion was so named because of the French name S. Martin d'été or le bouillant (boiling, i.e. in the hot season) to distinguish his summer feast day on 4 July from his winter feast day of Martinmas on 11 November.

The weather on 4 July was supposed to be prophetic, a bit like St Swithin's Day.

The traditional saying about a mild midwinter, *A green yule maks a full kirkyaird*, is, however, firmly grounded in common sense. There is nothing like a few good crisp frosts to kill off the harmful bugs.

Local Signs

In a country of mountains, lochs and rivers, with the Gulf Stream to the west and Siberia to the north-east, many areas have their own microclimate and the appearance of mist on the nearest hill may be much more reliable than the national weather forecast.

The Sidlaw Hills have their own rhyme:
> *Whan Craigowl pits on his cowl,*
> *And Coolie Law his hood,*
> *The fowk o Lundie may look dool,*
> *For the day'll no be good.*

(Traditional)

The Fife Hills have theirs too:

When Falkland Hill pits on his cap,

The Howe o Fife will get a drap,

And when the Bishop [one of the hills] *draws his*
cowl,

Luik oot for wind and weather foul!

(Traditional)

And Lochnagar:

"Fin yon fite Mounth frae sna be clear, the day o
doom is drawin near," quo Grannie in an uncannie
vyce. An sae I hid tae hear tell that the Fite Mounth
wis Lochnagar, an that he aye cairriet a wee pucklie
snaa at his bosie, an that if iver yon bosie tint its
snaa the warld wid cam tae its eyn

["When that white mountain from snow be clear,
the day of doom is drawing near," said Grannie in
an uncanny voice. And so I had to hear tell that the
White Mounth was Lochnagar, and that he always
carried a little bit of snow in his bosom, and if ever

[118]

that bosom lost its snow the world would come to
its end]

(SHEENA BLACKHALL *A Gey Dour Bitch* in
The Tower Quarters 2002)

However good we get at predicting the weather, it can
still sometimes take us by surprise and extremes of
weather can catch us unawares.

7 Lore

Some Facts and Figures

Scotland's weather may be variable but it is usually temperate. Rainfall may be higher over the West Highlands, but the east coast is no wetter than other parts of Britain. The Atlantic coast benefits from the warmth of the Gulf Stream and palm trees grow happily along the seafront at Plockton.

Even in winter, there is not usually a great deal of snow at low level, although a few Highland roads are notorious for being blocked. Snow can be expected to lie between ten days a year at sea level to seven months of the year on the top of the highest peaks. On 12 March 1947, an exceptional year, drifts more than 7 metres deep were recorded in the highlands of Scotland.

The lowest recorded temperature is -27.2 °C (17 °F) at Braemar on 10 January 1982 and 11 February 1895 and at Altnaharra on 30 December 1995.

The fastest recorded gust of wind reached 150 knots (173 mph) at Cairngorm Automatic Weather Station on 20 March 1986. The windiest places are the Western Isles, the North-West coast and Orkney and Shetland. They typically endure up to thirty days of gale per year. The maximum rainfall recorded in a day is 238 mm at Loch Lomond on 17 January 1974.

On the longest day, Lerwick has four more hours

of daylight than London, but on the shortest day, there are only six hours of daylight and the sun rises only 10 degrees above the horizon. The most bright sunshine in a month was 329 hours at Tiree in May 1946 and May 1975. The lowest number of sunny days in a month was 0.6 hours at Cape Wrath in January 1983.

Tornados – these are quite rare and used to be attributed to witchcraft, but in the tornado recorded in Annandale on 22 February 2006 there was a dramatic turn of events. The report in the local newspaper, the *Annandale Observer* (24 February 2006), records that Toss, a border collie, had an amazing escape. His owner recounted what happened:

> *Toss was chained to the kennel and they were both sucked up in the air. The kennel ended up on top of a wall and I found him still chained but OK on the other side from where he had been.*

Talk about giving a dog a bad name!

The Tay Bridge Disaster – on 28 December 1879, the railway bridge over the River Tay between Fife and Dundee gave way as the train from Edinburgh was passing over it. There had been concern among regular passengers about the condition of the bridge for some time and when it was subjected to a Force 10–11 gale, it collapsed with the loss of over seventy-five lives. The story is told by William McGonigal, Scotland's most celebrated bad poet:

'Twas about seven o'clock at night,
And the wind it blew with all its might,
And the rain came pouring down,
And the dark clouds seem'd to frown,
And the Demon of the air seem'd to say –
"I'll blow down the Bridge of Tay."
When the train left Edinburgh
The passengers' hearts were light and felt no sorrow,
But Boreas blew a terrific gale,
Which made their hearts for to quail,
And many of the passengers with fear did say –

"I hope God will send us safe across the Bridge of
      Tay."
But when the train came near to Wormit Bay,
Boreas he did loud and angry bray,
And shook the central girders of the Bridge of Tay
On the last Sabbath day of 1879,
Which will be remember'd for a very long time.
[. . .]
It must have been an awful sight,
To witness in the dusky moonlight,
While the Storm Fiend did laugh, and angry did
      bray,
Along the Railway Bridge of the Silv'ry Tay,
Oh! ill-fated Bridge of the Silv'ry Tay,
I must now conclude my lay
By telling the world fearlessly without the least
      dismay,
That your central girders would not have given way,
At least many sensible men do say,
Had they been supported on each side with
      buttresses,

At least many sensible men confesses,
For the stronger we our houses do build,
The less chance we have of being killed.

The Eyemouth Disaster – in a severe storm on 14 October 1881, 189 fishermen died, most of them from the village of Eyemouth in South-East Scotland. This was the worst fishing disaster Scotland has known. Within sight of the shore, the boats came to grief on the Hurkar Rocks.

The Moray Firth Disaster – on 18 August 1848, about 800 boats set out in good weather from many of the fishing towns and villages in North-East Scotland. During the night, a sudden and violent deterioration in the weather was responsible for the loss of 124 boats.

Gales on Shetland – the average January on Shetland has eight gale days, but in 1993 there were twenty-five gale days, ten of which saw storm-force or hurricane-force winds.

Storms on Orkney – on 15 January 1952 a terrific storm with 120mph winds swept Orkney. Although families were made homeless, there was no loss of human life. Hens fared less well. and not only were henhouses destroyed but many hens were killed as well. One henhouse was even carried out to sea with its occupants still inside.

The Great Storm of 1953 – the storm that hit Scotland on 31 January and 1 February 1953 was the worst in living memory. England and the Netherlands were also badly affected, with much loss of life. *The Princess Victoria*, the ferry sailing between Stranraer in south-west Scotland and Larne in Northern Ireland, sank with the loss of 133 lives and only 41 survivors. Rescue attempts were hampered by hurricane-force winds and blinding squalls of sleet. David Broadfoot, the radio operator, was posthumously awarded the George Cross for staying at his post until the ship sank within sight of the Irish coast.

Findhorn's misfortunes – the attractive village of Findhorn has suffered more than most from weather. There is evidence of an original village in existence in 1189 but as a result of storms in the seventeenth century, this village was buried by sand dunes. A new village was built which was in turn destroyed by flooding in 1701. Third time lucky?

The Grey Man of Ben Macdhui – a mystery lurks on the summit of Scotland's second-highest mountain. There have been many reports by climbers and hill-walkers who have heard the sound of footsteps behind them and have even seen a large grey figure. The experience is usually accompanied by feelings of panic. Does Scotland have its very own Yeti or Bigfoot?

Ben Macdhui is far too dangerous to be chased off in a panic in poor visibility. So if you do meet the Grey Man, take comfort from the fact that it is almost certainly a Brocken spectre, so named after the Brocken in the Harz Mountains in Germany.

The Brocken spectre is nothing more threatening than the shadow of the climber on the mist. So do not panic. Wait until the mist clears and you can make your way down in safety but if, while you are waiting, the Grey Man of Ben Macdhui engages you in conversation, be sure to let us know.

The Cailleach – Queen of the Winter.

In her highland cave, she imprisons the Maiden of Spring who, fortunately, always manages to escape, even if she is a little later in succeeding some years than others, and brings with her the first signs of Spring to celebrate at the Celtic festival of Imbolc. The Cailleach does not completely lose her power until Beltane (around 1 May) at which time she hides her staff under a gorse bush or holly bush and turns to stone. You must have noticed these single standing stones, solitary in fields or on heathland. At Samhain (November), the Cailleach is reborn and, taking up her staff again, she stalks the earth, frosting plants and bringing snow.

She is easily recognisable from her blue face and single eye but, like so many others of these ancient gods and goddesses, she is a shape changer and can appear as a beautiful woman to deceive the unwary.

Epilogue

The unpredictability of the Scottish weather is its greatest advantage. If the weather is bad, it won't stay that way for long. We rarely suffer from prolonged heatwaves and, even at the height of summer, grass is usually fresh and green. Our cities have extremely good air quality and, at least in the Lowlands, roads are only affected by snow for a few days most years. In a country of breath-taking scenery, every change of weather shows the landscape or seascape in new lights and new atmospheres.

The weather provides an unending topic of conversation. For an island nation which has traditionally relied on farming and fishing (although fishing is now sadly curtailed), the weather is a matter of vital importance. Most of the time we complain about it, but if we are away for any length of time, we miss – even

more than Scotch pies, mince and tatties and the sound
of oor ain tongue – our weather.

As Billy Connolly said, *There is no such thing as bad
weather, just the wrong clothes*. At least if it Is raining or
snowing, there are no midgies about. Every cloud has a
silver lining. And always remember:

> *The dowfiest day has aye the sun ayont it, an' the
> wather-gleam is aye the bonnier for the mornin's
> rain.*

(A. J. B. PATERSON *A Mist from Yarrow* 1896)